George Bailey Loring

Speech of Hon. George B. Loring

President of the Massachusetts Senate

George Bailey Loring

Speech of Hon. George B. Loring
President of the Massachusetts Senate

ISBN/EAN: 9783337175108

Printed in Europe, USA, Canada, Australia, Japan

Cover: Foto ©Suzi / pixelio.de

More available books at **www.hansebooks.com**

SPEECH

OF

HON. GEORGE B. LORING,

President of the Massachusetts Senate,

ON THE

QUESTION OF RESCINDING THE RESOLVE OF DEC. 18, 1872,

RELATING TO

HON. CHARLES SUMNER'S PROPOSITION WITH REGARD TO THE ARMY REGISTER AND REGIMENTAL COLORS.

JANUARY 30, 1874.

BOSTON:

WRIGHT & POTTER, STATE PRINTERS,

CORNER OF MILK AND FEDERAL STREETS.

1874.

SPEECH.

Mr. President :—

I ask the indulgence of the Senate while I discuss a question which has assumed an unexpected importance, and has come at last to involve the profound interest of a large class of the thoughtful and earnest people of this Commonwealth. A proposition made by Charles Sumner, in the Senate of the United States, early in the war of the Rebellion, and renewed when peace had so long spread over the land that the path of war was nearly obliterated, has given rise to a controversy which has been attended by unusual warmth of feeling on both sides. The friends of Mr. Sumner,—a long-tried, sincere and devoted body of political reformers, —filling every walk in life, from the student in his closet to the mechanic and laborer, who, for a quarter of a century, have caught their political inspiration from his burning words, feel that he has been censured without cause; and feel it deeply. The critics of Mr. Sumner (for I will not call all those who differ from him on the question before us, his enemies) are equally earnest in their belief that he has lost sight of his obligations to the best sentiment of the Commonwealth, and to that self-sacrificing valor which saved her and the country in the hour of trial. In the midst of this excitement, Mr. Sumner, himself, has been very freely handled. His long political career has been explored and discussed. His characteristics have been portrayed in striking lines. This very proposition with regard to army registers and regimental colors, which, had it originated with almost any other one of our public men, would have caused but little comment and hardly a ripple of feeling, has been mis-stated, magnified and distorted, until the true greatness of the author is lost sight of, and he is made rather an object of wonder than of admiration.

Now, sir, the prosperity and welfare of this Commonwealth are dear to us all. We are met within these walls to see that her institutions of learning and religion are guarded with a jeal-

ous care. For the comfort of the unfortunate
and the reformation of the erring, this assembly
is pledged to devote itself wisely and humanely.
It is understood throughout our borders that
every citizen may find here protection for those
rights which are guaranteed him by a free constitution. If there is a wrong, we are expected
to redress it; if there are any suffering from op-
pression and injustice, they turn to us for aid.
And I cannot for a moment doubt, that every
member of this body is impressed with a sense
of the obligations which he owes to an educated
and moral constituency, who sent him here, and
to that Commonwealth whose honorable record
appeals to him continually, to exercise his best
faculties for her future honor and prosperity.
But, foremost among all those questions which
bear upon the high tone and well-being of the
State, stands the consideration which the State
herself is to bestow upon those who have made
her truly great. A pseudo-republic may afford
to be ungrateful; a true republic cannot. Her
wise and brave and honest men are her strength;
and her capacity to produce the wise, the brave
and the honest, is the measure of her greatness.
A people who would preserve their power, and

who would so maintain themselves as to send
forth from their own ranks those who can guide
the State and preserve her institutions, and de-
velop her wealth and resources, are bound to be
generous as well as just, grateful as well as
exalted, forgiving as well as watchful,—as much
more proud of their great sons than the Roman
matron was of hers, as the lofty sentiment of a
high-toned community may be grander than mere
personal pride. That this is the animating sentiment of this Commonwealth and this country, I
cannot for a moment doubt. I think I see all
through the past, and in the passing events of
our own day, that it is public virtue alone that
has reached true public greatness; and that at
the hands of an educated and discriminating
people it has not failed to receive its high re-
ward. Eccentricity and weakness may have cast
a momentary shadow on the path of many whom
we call great, and who have secured high places
in our annals; but let us remember with pride
and satisfaction that the shadow has been but
momentary, and that thus far the people have
wisely discriminated between mistaken judgment
and the work of innate depravity. If we still
expect to multiply our great accomplishments,

we must cherish our great sons, remembering
that we can preserve their humility by kindly
consideration, and lash them into arrogance by
injustice and wrong. From our people has
sprung already a large store. of intellectual and
moral greatness,—poets and orators and schol-
ars,—jurists and historians and divines,—philoso-
phers who have made this State a home for the
masters of science,—wise old age and chivalrous
youth,—statesmen who have performed high service—soldiers who have an honorable record,—
and martyred soldiers, who, dying on the battle-
field, rose to a youthful and radiant immortality,
and inscribed an inspiring chapter on the history
of their country. In this illustrious company
Charles Sumner has secured a high place, offer-
ing as his tribute to his Commonwealth and his
country, a constant and persevering effort to
purify and elevate our institutions,—an example
of integrity and high purpose worthy of all
imitation,—a long, direct, and unswerving career
as a statesman,—and a continued popular support, almost unequalled in political history, and
the natural result of an unwavering endeavor to
be true to the best principles of republican state
and society, laid down by those who founded

our government. Whatever may be his faults, this at least is his fame. And I think I do not assume too much—not more than every citizen of this Commonwealth would freely grant—when I ask that this should be considered, in our judgment upon any public act or expression of his which may not receive our entire and immediate approval.

But, sir, what is the precise issue?

As the civil war, from which we have but recently emerged, went on, and at its close, questions of greater or less importance continually arose with regard to the arrangement of our civil and military affairs, and the reconstruction of our republic. Among these questions the inquiry naturally came up as to how far the memories of the conflict should be perpetuated,—a question new to us, but one which had been considered and adjusted by every nation, ancient and modern, in which civil conflict had been carried on. It was in this connection, that on May 8th, 1862, Mr. Sumner offered, in the United States Senate, the following Resolve:—

Resolved, That in the efforts now making for the restoration of the Union, and the establishment of peace throughout the country, it is inexpedient that the names of the victories obtained over our fellow-citizens should be placed on the regimental colors of the United States.

It was at this time that the struggles of the war were the severest. The calls upon Massachusetts for troops were incessant. Washington was threatened. Stonewall Jackson was dashing in triumphant career through Virginia. The anxiety was great; and all the energies of this Commonwealth were put forth to respond to the call of the Federal government. Then it was that Governor Andrew declared: "But if the president will sustain Gen. Hunter,—recognize all men, even black men, as legally capable of that loyalty the blacks are waiting to manifest, and let them fight with God and human nature on their side,—the roads will swarm, if need be, with multitudes whom New England would pour out to obey your call." The people had begun to discover the true meaning of the war. During the few months, about this time, nearly five thousand men had been recruited for three years' service, and sent to the front; also Cook's battery; three companies of unattached cavalry; three companies of infantry to complete the organization of the Twenty-ninth Regiment; the Twenty-eighth Regiment; the Sixth Battery; the Thirty-first Regiment; seven companies, comprising what was known as the Fort Warren Battalion, and afterwards the Thirty-second Regiment which were sent forward to the Army of the Potomac, and two companies for the Fourteenth Regiment, afterwards changed to the First Massachusetts Heavy Artillery. This was the sentiment which animated Massachusetts at this time,—a period in which McClellan was conducting the Peninsular campaign; and Banks was struggling in the Valley; and it was in the midst of these hard and discouraging days, and of the demands upon the patriotism of his own State, that Mr. Sumner, with sublime confidence in the result, and seeing afar off the victorious termination, offered the Resolve which I have just read.

I look in vain for any censure, direct or implied, or any reflection cast upon him by legislature or people, on account of this proposition which he felt called upon to make in those early days of the war. The armies from North Carolina to Mississippi were filled with Massachusetts men; but they did not take him to task for his

utterance. The governor of Massachusetts was
called on for reinforcements continually; and he
only asked that the issue might be made high
enough by the administration, and not that Mr.
Sumner might be suppressed, in order to fill
the roads with the advancing men of New England. The Republican State Convention met at
Worcester on the 10th of September following.
Governor Andrew was renominated; a letter was
read from Mr. Sumner, earnestly advocating
emancipation as the issue of the war; and Resolutions were adopted, indorsing his views and
favoring his reëlection to the United States Senate. The legislature met on the 7th of January
following. I look in vain upon its journals for
any censure of Mr. Sumner, for his Resolve of
May 8th, 1862. On the contrary, I find him re-
elected for a third term to the United States
Senate, and that, too, by a legislature whose attention was largely drawn towards the soldiers
of the Union army, and which passed an Act
appropriating the sum of ten thousand dollars,
for the benefit of the Discharged Soldiers' Home;
—an Act authorizing state aid to be paid to
families of drafted men the same as to families
of volunteers;—a Resolve in grateful acknowledg-

ment of the services rendered by our soldiers in the war;—an Act providing for the payment by the State of the pay due to the soldiers by the Federal government;—an Act authorizing the governor to pay bounties, not to exceed fifty dollars each, to volunteers;—an Act appropriating twenty thousand dollars for the maintenance of agencies out of the Commonwealth, as the governor may find needful, for the aid of sick and wounded or distressed Massachusetts soldiers;— and an Act authorizing cities and towns to raise money by taxation for the support of the families of deceased soldiers; also, families of soldiers discharged for disability. Why, sir, this was a legislature especially devoted to the soldier; but I find no complaint of Mr. Sumner's Resolve on its journal.

The war ended; the armies disbanded; the soldiers returned to their homes; the torn and tattered and honored and historic battle-flags were gathered into the archives of each State which had sent them forth; the reconciliations of peace went on; the fruits of the war were gathered in; a grateful people poured forth their tributes in every form to the loyal soldier; the reconstruction of the government was perfected;

and a restored and strengthened American Republic had taken its place among the nations of the earth. It was in *this* state of affairs that Mr. Sumner, still true to a sentiment which had been tacitly accepted on a former occasion, and which had been universally adopted in the adjustment of public difficulties, introduced into the Senate of the United States, on the 2d of December, 1872, the following:—

A BILL TO REGULATE THE ARMY REGISTER AND THE REGIMENTAL COLORS OF THE UNITED STATES.

Whereas, The national unity and good-will among fellow-citizens can be assured only through oblivion of past differences, and it is contrary to the usage of civilized nations to perpetuate the memory of civil war; therefore,

Be it enacted by the Senate and House of Representatives of the United States of America in Congress assembled, That the names of battles with fellow-citizens shall not be continued in the Army Register, or placed on the regimental colors of the United States.

The introduction of this bill, a counterpart of the Resolve of May 8th, 1862, and brought forward, as I have every reason to know, at the suggestion of an ardent friend of the national administration, as a final measure of reconciliation, gave rise to a warm debate in the extra session of the Massachusetts legislature in December, 1872, which resulted in the adoption of the following Resolutions, December 18th, 1872 :—

RESOLUTIONS RELATING TO THE BILL PENDING IN CONGRESS CONCERNING THE ARMY REGISTERS AND THE NATIONAL FLAGS.

Resolved, By the Senate and House of Representatives in General Court assembled:

That, Whereas, A bill has been introduced into the Senate of the United States by a senator of Massachusetts, providing "that the names of battles with fellow-citizens shall not be continued in the Army Register, or placed on the regimental colors of the United States"; and

Whereas, The passage of such a bill would be an insult to the loyal soldiery of the nation, and depreciate their grand achievements in the late Rebellion; therefore,

Resolved, That such legislation meets the unqualified condemnation of the people of this Commonwealth.

Resolved, That the governor be requested to forward to our senators and representatives in Congress copies of these resolutions.

It is these Resolutions which we are requested to rescind, or expunge, or in some way remove, or offset, by a legislative expression of our own. In advocating this I do not think it necessary to characterize the Resolutions passed by a former legislature by any very definite phrase. It is

claimed for them that they do not refer to Mr.
Sumner in person, and that they do not cast
censure on him for any act committed by him
in the Senate of the United States. It is enough
for me to know that they would never have been
adopted but for his bill relating to the Army
Register and regimental colors, and that they
either refer to that bill and to him as the author,
or else they refer to nothing and nobody. If they
refer to him, I think they ought to be rescinded
or expunged; if they do not refer to him and
his bill, they certainly ought to be rescinded, as
null and void, and occupying, without meaning
or object, a place on the journals of the two
branches of the legislature. Neither do I care
to discuss the wholesale statement that "such
legislation" as that proposed by Mr. Sumner,
"meets the unqualified condemnation of the people of the Commonwealth." The flood of peti-
tions which has been poured in upon the legislature during this session and the last preceding,
is a sufficient answer to this assumption. But I
do desire to call the attention of senators to the
danger which always attends the adoption of
Resolutions which relate chiefly to personal politics, by a legislative body convened to perform

the legitimate legislative business of a Commonwealth. To the indorsement of general principles, or of a policy of government, which may
become a part of the fundamental law of the
land in a great crisis, there can be no objection.
Our fathers set us an example of this which we
can well afford to follow, when they filled their
halls of legislation with representatives instructed
by their constituents to support the independence
of the rising republic. But neither sound wisdom nor experience teaches us, that a legislature
can with safety and a due regard for its dignity
and duty, plunge into personal political controversies, which are always likely to end in a way
not anticipated by those who are engaged in
them. The history of Resolutions of censure in
this country is not encouraging.

With this feeling in my mind I cannot for a
moment entertain the idea that the rescinding of
a Resolution of this description is in any way an
insult to the legislative body which passed it.
It stands as an expression of opinion merely,—is
expunged or rescinded as an expression of
opinion,—and can be renewed and adopted as
still another expression of what may or may not
be a popular sentiment. No Resolution has ever

yet been expunged from an American legislative journal that I am aware of, for the purpose of insulting its authors in a previous legislature; but as what the expungers thought an act of justice to those who were censured. No senator at this board in voting to rescind, proposes to cast a reflection upon those who adopted the Resolves which he wishes to remove. Every man is willing to allow that they were considered by their supporters to be an honest expression of the opinion of the hour when they were adopted. But believing as we do that the time has arrived, when, viewed in the light of the present, they neither set forth the spirit and intention of Mr. Sumner, nor express the popular voice, they ought to be rescinded, we assume that the legislature which adopted them is still open to conviction, and that we can express our views without a shadow of insult or reproach. We can repeal an Act without censure or reflection; why, then, can we not rescind a Resolve?

And now a word with regard to our constitutional right to rescind or expunge these Resolutions, which has frequently been called in question. I had supposed that if this point had been settled in no other way, it had been settled by well known and remarkable precedents, both in the legislature of this Commonwealth and of the nation.

Every student of the political history of Massachusetts is familiar with the Resolution which passed this body on the 15th of June, 1813, not only declining in substance to rejoice over the victory of the U. S. ship Hornet over His Britannic Majesty's ship Peacock,—a victory which cost the country the life of one of her bravest officers,—but also reflecting severely on the war in which that victory was won. We have no record, that I am aware of, of the vote by which this Resolve passed the Senate. But we do know that it was looked upon at that time as a political party measure in the strictest sense, and that an early struggle commenced to expunge it from the journal. This effort commenced February 10th, 1814, on a motion of Mr. Holmes, to erase the Resolve; and the motion was defeated by a vote of 20 to 8, the yeas and nays on the question showing a strictly party vote. The effort to expunge, however, was not abandoned; and on the 23d of January, 1824, the Hon. Seth Sprague, senator from Plymouth, a descendant of the Pilgrims, a sincere and manly representative of their highest virtues, an early advocate of human freedom, an ardent patriot and a wise legislator, moved the following Resolution, which, with an elaborate preamble, was adopted by a vote of 22 to 15:—

Resolved, That the resolve aforesaid of the 15th day of June, A. D. 1813, and the preamble thereof be and the same are hereby expunged from the journals of the Senate.

Every student of the political history of our country is familiar with the long and violent contest in the United States Senate, over the proposition of Mr. Benton to expunge from the journal of that body the Resolution adopted March 28, 1834, charging upon President Jackson, that, " in the late executive proceedings in relation to the public revenue, he had assumed upon himself authority and power not conferred by the Constitution and the laws, but in derogation of both." For more than three years the contest raged from time to time in one form or another. The opponents of the administration, driven from one point to another, clamored at last for the integrity of the journal. They were ready to " rescind, reverse and make null and void," but not to "expunge." It was claimed that the Senate was required by the Constitution to "keep" a journal, and that the word "keep" meant to "preserve." To this it was replied that, "To keep a journal is to write down daily what you do. For the Senate to keep a journal is to cause to be written down every day the account of its proceedings; and having done that, the constitutional injunction is satisfied. The Constitution was satisfied by entering this criminating Resolution on the journal; it will be equally satisfied by entering the expunging Resolution on the same journal. In each case the Senate keeps a journal of its own proceedings." And this argument was deemed to be satisfactory, sustained as it was by parliamentary precedent in this country and in England, in the Massachusetts Senate and in the British Parliament. And so in reference to the condemnatory Resolve of March 28, 1834, the following Resolve was adopted:—

Resolved, That the said resolve be expunged from the journal; and, for the purpose, that the Secretary of the Senate, at such time as the Senate may appoint, shall bring the manuscript journal of the session of 1833–34 into the Senate, and, in the presence of the

Senate, draw black lines round the said resolve, and write across the face thereof, in strong letters, the following words: "Expunged by order of the Senate this 16th day of March, 1837."

The order of the Senate was carried out, and there the "strong letters" remain to this day.

The student of English political and parliamentary history is familiar with the case of the Middlesex election, in which the Resolution to expel John Wilkes was expunged from the journal. The contest over this expunging Resolve commenced in 1769, and continued until 1782, when it was adopted as follows:—

Resolved, That the resolution of the House of the 17th of February, 1769, "that John Wilkes, Esq., having been in this session of Parliament expelled this House, was, and is, incapable of being elected a member to serve in the present Parliament," be expunged from the journals of this House as being subversive of the rights of the whole body of electors of this kingdom.

And this Resolve was ultimately adopted in the House of Commons by a vote of three to one, supported as it was by Burke, and Fox, and all the friends of American Independence and human freedom in that august body.

Why, sir, it seems to me that by these precedents, in establishing which this very body of
which we are members has performed a part,
we may not only learn what our constitutional
rights and powers .are, but what has become the
parliamentary form in which dissent from recorded Resolves may find its way upon the
journals of legislative bodies. The word " expunge " has become as familiar almost as the
word " resolve "; and I trust it will be accepted
in relation to Resolutions, as the word " repeal "
is accepted in relation to Acts and Statutes. So
much for our powers.

I suppose, Mr. President, the character of
every legislative measure is to be estimated from
the results of its operation, and in order that
senators may understand the exact purport of
the bill introduced by Mr. Sumner with regard
to the Army Register and regimental colors, I
will endeavor to set forth the effect it would
produce were it to become a law. The Resolutions adopted by our predecessors in these halls
declared that " the passage of such a bill would
be an insult to the loyal soldiery of the nation,
and depreciate their grand achievements in the
late Rebellion." We have been told in terms so

earnest that we could not for a moment doubt the sincerity of those who stated them, that the bill was a blow at the maimed and wounded soldier, whose presence reminds us continually of the desperate severity of the struggle with the Rebellion, and a reflection upon the memory of those who laid down their lives in that bloody conflict. We have been repeatedly and solemnly warned that this is but the beginning of a movement which will end in the obliteration of all mementos of the war, and in the overthrow of those monuments which have arisen in every loyal village of our land, to record the valor of our sons, and to teach the lesson of patriotic devotion to those who come after us,—those soldiers' monuments, in the erection of which the grateful hearts of our people have inspired an honorable liberality, and in the dedication of which some of us have again and again offered our best thoughts and sentiments, feeling that no tribute could be great enough for the sacred service. It has been urged upon us that this is but a signal for the soldier to retire from the front and be forgotten. Now, sir, all this may be true. But where and how is this work to begin? The bill deals entirely with the Army

Register and the regimental colors of the Regular Army of the United States. At the present time the army consists of:

CAVALRY—Ten regiments, four of which were organized by Act of Congress July 28, 1866, and of course took no part in the civil war.

ARTILLERY—Five regiments, the First having been engaged at the Heights of Queenstown, October 13, 1812, in the Florida and Mexican wars, and in the civil war until the autumn of 1864; the Second, beginning at Chippewa, and ending at Cedar Creek; the Third having been engaged at Chippewa, in the Florida and Mexican wars, and in the civil war to the battle of Laurel Hill, October 7th, 1864; the Fourth dating also from Chippewa to Hatcher's Run, March, 1865; and the Fifth from Bull Run to Petersburg, April, 1865.

INFANTRY—Twenty-five regiments, two of which have been organized since the war, many of the remainder dating from the war of 1812. Ten of these regiments of infantry have been re-organized by consolidation of other regiments, many of them not having taken part under their present names in engagements which are credited

to them, but which belong to those regiments of
which they are composed.

It seems, therefore, that there are forty regiments of cavalry, artillery and infantry combined,
many of which took no part in the civil war,
and many others of which have been re-organized since that conflict ended. It is the regimental colors of these regiments alone which
can possibly be affected by the bill of Mr. Sumner, and which are in any way directly inter-
ested in the issue. To this extent can the question be carried—no more. To about thirty
regiments of the regular army, composed of
men from all sections of the country, commanded, or to be commanded, by officers selected
without regard to birthplace and parentage, the
suggestion of Mr. Sumner is alone applicable.
He desires that the colors which float over them
shall remind them only of that united nationality
in whose service they are engaged, and of those
battles in which the entire country had a mutual
and undivided interest. Can we not imagine
that in his mind the thronging regiments of a
loyal North, to whom belongs the glory of the
war, stand before the world in a very different
light from that presented by a regular army

organized without reference to State or section? The seventy-eight regiments which Massachusetts sent to the war,—can he place them in history exactly by the side of the heroes of Chepulte-pec and Okee-cho-bee? Can you, sir? It was as Northern regiments that they all, volunteers and regulars, fought for the Union; and those that continued in the service became national, when the war ended and the Union was pre-served. American success and renown in the civil war are not based on the achievements of a standing army. While the regular regiments did their duty well in that great conflict, the grand accomplishments of the war are due to that vast body of citizens, once a citizen-soldiery, now filling every walk in civil life,—whose tat-tered regimental colors are preserved as trophies of their valor in the archives of every loyal State, and whose glory cannot be taken from them. On their regimental colors, on the monuments erected in memory of their dead comrades, on many a radiant page of their country's history which will be cherished and pondered long after army registers shall all be forgotten, will be found the hallowed names of those conflicts which preserved and purified the nation. To the heroes of those conflicts belong still the tattered battle-flags ; to them belong the memorial days ; to them belong the monuments ; to them belong the historical renown,—which no Act of Congress can take from them, and of which, thank God, no son of Massachusetts has ever yet desired to deprive them.

And, then, why should Mr. Sumner be engaged in insulting "the loyal soldiery of the nation"? The relations which history has established between him and them are most intimate. He must know that but for them the efforts of his long public service would have availed nothing; his prayer for freedom and humanity would have been in vain. He must know that their victory was his victory. And they must know that when they look for the crowning glory of their toil and suffering on the field of battle, they find it in the triumph which their victorious swords secured for the principles of free government, and civil rights, and social equality, which Charles Sumner has proclaimed and defended with unequalled constancy and devotion. Strip from your banners, loyal soldiers of the North! the doctrines which he laid down as the true object of the war,—roll back the tide of freedom which flowed on with your advancing and victorious ranks,—wipe out the Emancipation Proclamation, and restore the almost forgotten statutes for which the war began,—and mark then the shadow which would fall upon the page whereon your heroic deeds are recorded. The war was great in its military achievements; but greater still in the great reform which it accomplished. And I cannot believe that the soldiers who won that military renown, will hasten to condemn the foremost advocate of those doctrines, which shed peculiar lustre on their deeds of valor, or will be ready to believe that by thought, or word, or deed, he would detract from the position they have honorably won.

I think, sir, I can find other motives, and very different from those attributed to him, which may have led Mr. Sumner to make his proposition early in the war, and to renew it in times of peace. While he stands foremost among the progressive statesmen of our country, he is also strongly attracted by great historic events and great historic precedents. To his mind the passage of time has evidently established certain well-worn channels in which

the currents of historical events may naturally
flow; and to him, as to every student, there
is a certain charm about historical correspond-
ences, and analogies, and precedents, and poli-
cies, and characters, as they appear from age
to age. He had before him that striking and
mysterious sensitiveness which led the Romans
to preserve all possible silence over their civil
wars, and decreed that Cæsar should not
triumph over Pompey, even after he had conquered him. So, too, the record of the British
army had impressed him, as it will us. Nothing need be said of the wars of the Roses
or of the Commonwealth, because the regiments of that day do not now exist. But
Culloden was one of the most important battles
in British history, for the Stuart dynasty received there its final defeat. The regiments
in that field, commanded by the king's son,
still exist; but this battle is not on their
colors. How could it be without annoyance
to every Scotchman? Our Revolutionary war
was to England a "civil war,"—so called continually, and so treated,—inasmuch as not one
of its numerous battles figures on any regimental colors; while the battles of the war of

1812—Niagara, Detroit, Bladensburg,—are to be
found in the British Army List and on the
regimental colors; and this because in this
latter war the United States were a foreign
power. The celebrated 4th, or King's Own
Regiment, which so annoyed our fathers and
played an important part during the siege of
Boston, displays not a single name of a revolutionary battle; but rejoices in the glory
shed upon it by Corunna, and Badajos, and
Salamanca, and Vittoria, and St. Sebastian,
and the Peninsula, and Bladensburg, and
Waterloo, and Alma, and Inkermann and Sebastopol. The 5th regiment, which was here
during the Revolutionary war, glories in a long
list from Corunna to Lucknow; the 35th re-
cords its deeds in Hindostan and the Peninsula; so the 33d, the Duke of Wellington's,
remembers with pride Waterloo, Alma and
Sebastopol; the 42d the Royal Highland, *Nemo
me impune lacessit*, marches with firmer step
beneath the names of Pyrenees, Corunna, Tou-
louse, Waterloo, and Lucknow; and the 44th
turns its eye upon Salamanca, and is reminded
of that fiery time when Marmont was defeated
by the Iron Duke, and acknowledged that no

Marshal of France could resist his impetuosity
and skill. India, the Peninsula, the Crimea,
the Continent, all furnish names to adorn the
regimental colors of these historic bands which
I have enumerated; but nowhere on these colors,
or in the British Army List, do I find the names
of Bunker Hill, and Saratoga, and Camden, and
Long Island, and Guilford, and Monmouth, and
Yorktown, battles of the British soldiers with
their brethren.

This English rule is followed in France. No
battle in civil war appears on any French flag.
The same is true in Prussia; nor has Austria any
battle with the Hungarians written on her colors.
The rule seems to be universal. No battle in civil
war can find a place on the regimental colors of a
united people. This is the lesson taught by history and by national example.

And may we not charge, moreover, the views
of Mr. Sumner on this matter partly to the
spirit of reconciliation, which has constituted
one of the most remarkable features of the
war and peace policy of the American government and people? In nothing has our republic manifested its conscious strength more than
in this. Without example or precedent we

have conquered insurgents, and then forgiven them. Whether this is due to the confidence which the American people feel in the vital energy and strength of their form of government, or to the elevating influence upon the popular mind of the great philanthropic results of the war, I will not undertake to say. But it has borne along with irresistible force statesmen and warriors and people alike, and forms a contrast to the policy and necessity of other nations in the midst of civil war, of which we have reason to be proud. As an evidence of innate strength it is unparalleled; as a test of that strength it should never be forgotten by all people endeavoring to found and maintain a free state. That general amnesty which has even opened the halls of Congress, and prepared the way to high seats in the national councils, for those who not long since were arrayed against the government,—what a problem will it furnish the future historian! That advice of our victorious general to the armed bands who surrendered to his superior power and skill, that they should retain their horses and return at once to their labor on the land which they had left for the battle-field,—what an example

it set to the conquerors of all coming time!
And would you learn the value of all this by
contrast? Turn, if you would, to the capture
of Monmouth after the battle of Sedgemoor;—
the last fight deserving the name of battle
that has been fought on English ground;—
Monmouth, discovered as he was at length, a
gaunt figure hidden in a ditch, his beard pre-
maturely gray, his appearance abject, his courage gone before the fate which in those days
awaited a conspirator. Follow him on his
weary journey to London, listen to his feeble
lamentation, and recall his painful and sicken-
ing death on the block, at the behests of a
king who had neither courage nor magnanimity
enough to spare him. You know the resem-
blance and the contrast in our own history.
Would you go still further? Remember the
fate of Lesley's men at Dunbar, exiled when
defeated by the Protector who betrayed a republic, and compare it with the wisdom of him
who conquered Lee's army before Richmond,
and, having saved a republic, advised the insurgents to return quietly to their homes. Would
you go further still? Remember, then, the republican butcheries at Satory, and mark the

5

gloom of that cold, gray winter morning when Rossel, the brilliant and accomplished, was shot down, a sacrifice to the fears of a sham republic. I hardly know which in after-time will be admired most, our vigorous prosecution of the war, or what John A. Andrew so nobly called our vigorous prosecution of peace. But of one thing I am sure,—that no word of mine shall ever discourage any American, high or low, in his endeavor to join the ranks of those who have labored to prove to the world that in a true republic, "the hour of triumph is the hour of magnanimity."

But I know I shall be reminded, as I have already been, that Mr. Sumner insisted most strenuously on confiscation and death as the punishment for treason, even while manifesting on other points a spirit of forgiveness and reconciliation. I agree; but I charge this again to the teachings of history. The law of the world almost with regard to treason and conspiracy was—"indemnity for the past and security for the future." "Rebels in arms are enemies," we have learned from all the fountains of constitutional law; and the natural inference was that persons arrayed for the overthrow of the government of the United States are crimi-

nals and enemies, because they set themselves up
traitorously against the government of their country. "The goods of enemies, as well those found
among us as those taken in war, shall be confiscated," said the highest legal authorities. In the
state trials in England we have been told that "no
country can ever be brought thoroughly under sub-
jection, if it is to be held that where there has been
a conquest, and no capitulation, the mere publica-
tion of a proclamation desiring the people to be
quiet and telling them that means would be re-
sorted to if they were not so, so far reduces the
country under civil rule that the army loses its
control, and the municipal courts acquire altogether
jurisdiction, so that every action of the officers in
the direction of military affairs is liable to their
cognizance." And we are disposed to be warned
thereby. We learn from Roman history that "confiscation is inseparable from war,"—a rule but little
known, it is true, in the better days of the republic,
but prevailing under the emperors; and that "it
was a distribution of bounty lands among the soldiers of Octavius, after the establishment of his
power, that drove Virgil from his paternal acres to
seek imperial favor at Rome." We know that confiscation was directed in Florence against Dante,

and in Holland against Grotius. By it William of
Normandy despoiled the Saxons of their lands and
divided them among his followers. In Germany,
during the period of theological conflicts, it was
often used among the Protestants. In Spain it
was applied to Moors and Jews. By the law of
England it was the inseparable incident of treason
—flourishing always in Ireland and Great Britain.
The scaffold always turned over to the government
the estate of its victim. In modern France, confiscation has played a conspicuous part. From August 10th, 1792, in the French Revolution, to 1801,
sales had been authorized to the amount of 2,560,-
000,000 francs. All Napoleon could do was to
reduce the list, and even he declared, when the
exempts returned and proceeded to cut down their
forests in order to strip the land and fill their pock-
ets, "We cannot allow the greatest enemies of the
republic, the defenders of old prejudices, to recover
their fortunes and despoil France." The confiscation of the property of Loyalists and Tories was a
part of the colonial work during our Revolution.
"Can we subsist," said the patriot Hawley to El-
bridge Gerry, July 17, 1776, "did any State ever
subsist, without exterminating traitors?" In almost all the thirteen original States, from 1778 to

1787, statutes of confiscation and the settlement of confiscated estates for the benefit of government were passed. Relief for all this was found in a recommendation by Congress "that the legislatures of the respective States should restore the estates, rights and property of real British subjects, and also of those who have borne arms against the United States." That confiscation was complete but few doubted. Jefferson, when Secretary of State, in a very able state paper sustained the policy of the United States Government, holding that the confiscation is complete by the passage of the Act of confiscation,—"both the title and the possession being diverted out of the former proprietor, and vested in the State." And the Supreme Court sustained him.

This is the lesson which history teaches us; and it is easy to see how, in the turmoil and difficulty of a vast insurrection, the accepted policy of every civilized nation, and our own declared theory should have appeared inevitable and necessary. The punishment of political offenders and state criminals has occupied a place in history alongside of the penalities imposed upon capital offences of every description; and it has had no relation whatever to those measures by which the masses of the people are to be reconciled, and the way prepared for their return to the blessings of peace and a united state after the convulsions of civil war. It remained for us in our own hard experience to teach mankind that the offences which attend political disturbances, and spring from political controversies and passions, cannot be attached to individuals alone; that oftentimes it is the people who lead, and not their agents, in the strife; and that a beneficent government can maintain itself better by magnanimity than by the terrors of confiscation and death, in which too often the innocent suffer with the guilty, and by which an undying sense of wrong is left as a legacy, and is accepted for generations as an inheritance. But all this we have been compelled to learn for ourselves. We had no teachers. And I should be sorry to believe that an able and exhaustive exposition of the law relating to political offenders, as laid down by jurists and statesmen of all ages, and accepted as the necessary attendant of the sword in civil convulsions, should be charged against any United States Senator as an evidence of a severity inappropriate to the land and the age in which we live, and inconsistent with the measures of moderation in which he has

taken conspicuous part. Nor can I understand
why an advocate of existing law and established
precedent should be denied the privilege of
smoothing the path of the innocent, while he feels
compelled to pass the guilty over to merited punishment. The American nation has laid down a
better law, and established a better penalty for
treason. Does any man suppose that Mr. Sumner
fails to accept this as one of the most Christian
acts of that country which he is proud to call his
own, and for whose dignity and elevation and
prosperity he has ever been diligent and watchful?
It seems to me, sir, easy to understand how as an
advocate of every measure of reconciliation, he
should also be allowed to define the penalty of
treason.

But, sir, assuming that Mr. Sumner, on the
matter immediately before us, is mistaken, and
that the policy of other nations with regard to
their army registers and regimental colors is not
acceptable to the American people, is his offence
really of such magnitude as to call for public censure from the highest assembly of the Commonwealth which he represents? We should not for-
get that legislative censure is a matter of deep and
profound import. It stands next in the scale to

impeachment. It properly applies to all delinquencies which fall short of those grave offences for which the Constitution provides an equivalent punishment. But these delinquencies are not to be hastily and thoughtlessly arraigned. Gross and wilful violation of the Constitution by a public servant, or a dangerous assumption of power, is easily classified and easily presented. But a distasteful judgment, a disappointing vote, an unexpected opinion, are not matters which come so near to moral turpitude, or a neglect of trust imposed, or any other unimpeachable offence, as to merit that form of rebuke which stands next to impeachment itself. Nothing but the possibility that a position assumed by a representative of the people may lead to disastrous results, if followed out to a legitimate conclusion, should subject that representative to popular rebuke or legislative censure, and then only as a warning or as an appeal which at the commencement of what might lead to severer measures, may be wise and judicious, and in fact useful. But legislative censure simply as an expression of difference of opinion is undoubtedly harsh, and may be unjust. Expressions of this sort apply properly to questions of general interest in which personal reputation is not involved.

Hitherto, Massachusetts has been extremely careful in legislative action of this kind; and in fact great care has been exercised in this respect in all her popular assemblies. Expressions of opinion by the press and the people have always been freely and liberally given. But the exercise of authority has been cautious and mild. The criticisms passed upon her public men have seldom taken the form of official declaration; owing, I doubt not, to a feeling that every man should have an opportunity for free and fair and unprejudiced discussion. This has always been allowed.

Few of us have forgotten, for instance, the remarkable, stirring and prophetic speech of Senator Sumner, at the Republican State Convention at Worcester, October 1, 1861. It was less than six months after the war began. It was less than three months after Congress had declared by formal Resolve that the war was conducted for the restoration of the Union and not for interference with the domestic institutions of any State. It was a convention of men controlling the politics of Massachusetts, possessed of the executive and the legislature, and supporting the

Federal administration then in power. Mr. Sumner's theme was "*Emancipation our best Weapon*"; and after having denounced slavery as the cause of the war, he exclaimed—"Two objects are before us, Union and Peace, each for the sake of the other, and both for the sake of the country; but without emancipation how can we expect either?" "Hearken not," said he, "to the voice of slavery, no matter what its tone of persuasion. It is the gigantic traitor and parricide, not for a moment to be trusted. Believe me, its friendship is more deadly than its enmity. If you are wise, prudent, economical, conservative, practical, you will strike quick and hard,—strike, too, where the blow will be most felt,—strike at the main-spring of the Rebellion. Strike in the name of the Union, which only in this way can be restored,—in the name of peace, which is vain without the Union,—and in the name of liberty, also, sure to bring both Peace and Union in her glorious train."

Think not that this speech was approved by the party to which Mr. Sumner belonged. It was not. "The convention certainly disavowed any intention of indorsing the fatal doctrines announced by Mr. Sumner," said a leading republican organ on the day after the speech was made. "His appearance this year was not in accordance with the wishes of those who do not follow his lead, but regard him as one of the most irrepressible impracticables of the party," said another. "We fear it is but an illustration of the mental perversity produced by entire absorption in a single aspect of a great question without regard to its manifold relations, and by the 'sacred animosity' which, too exclusively nourished, renders the best men reckless of means in the pursuit of what they consider the chief end of life," said another. "Charles Sumner's speech will be found on our first page to-day. We give it, not by way of approval, for it seems to us the worst speech that could be made," said another. Mr. Sumner had arrayed himself against the avowed policy of the republican party of that day, against the policy of the administration whose supporter he was expected to be in Congress, and against the expressed views of his political associates. But, dangerous as his doctrines were then thought to be, he received no legislative censure ; he was not severed from his party; he was allowed to discuss his views freely and fairly, and the discussion ended in such an overwhelming triumph of his doctrines that the whole country has accepted them, and the dispute has ended forever.

When a distinguished member of Congress from this State advocated financial views which were deemed worthy of special rejection by his own party, both in national and state convention, and were denounced by the press and on the platform in most unmeasured terms, he received still the party support to which his general views entitled him, and no man heard of legislative censure. His doctrines were rejected; but the freeman's right of debate was not denied him, nor was he condemned unheard.

When the great Massachusetts Senator who won for himself the proud title of the Defender of the Constitution, felt called upon to advocate doctrines which were obnoxious to a large part of the people of this Commonwealth, in the discharge of his duty as he understood it, during a severe crisis in our history, the press and the pulpit and the rostrum thundered against him; but the journals of the legislature contain no record of that stormy conflict which was quietly suppressed in these halls, where his voice had been so often heard, and where he so often received his civic crown.

When the administration of General Grant was laboring to establish the principle of arbitration for the adjustment of international difficulties, as a Christian substitute for war, and presented it to the people as the most honorable act in its domestic and foreign policy, you well know with what vigor and eloquence it was opposed here, and how silent a Republican legislature was with regard to that opposition. When the popular indignation was raging against an Act of Congress, increasing the salaries of a large number of public officials, Congressmen included, and the legislature was called upon to utter its protest against the obnoxious measure, have you forgotten how resolutely it refused to enter into the conflict? When a prominent and faithful member of Congress from this State, charged upon the administration in the early months of its existence, that its extravagance was ruining the country, and his utterances were used as a powerful weapon against his own party, a Republican legislature was silent. And the debate went on.

No, sir; our political history is full of incidents like these, in which opportunities occurred, and legitimate opportunities, too, as many were inclined to think, for legislative censure. But I look in vain for it. Massachusetts has learned to tolerate great freedom of opinion among her people; and to this grand purpose I trust she will adhere so long as she claims to be a free Commonwealth in a free Republic.

And now, Mr. President, I do indeed reproach myself for having occupied so much of the time of the Senate on a question which I suppose I ought to have considered settled in the minds of every senator at this board. I know how thoroughly it has been discussed; and perhaps I ought to have known that it was presumptuous in me to hope to add a single argument to the great mass already accumulated, or a particle of information to that already poured forth by abler lips than mine. But you will pardon me when I suggest that perhaps all the facts in the case had not been laid before the public mind, and that I may have thrown some light upon the true intent and meaning of Mr. Sumner's bill. I have no other desire than that a fair and candid verdict shall be passed upon his proposition. I must confess to a little anxiety that justice shall be done ere it is too late; for I am sure

that if this business is prolonged, and year after
year shall roll away, those who come after us
and proceed to the duty which we should perform, will not look back with entire satisfaction
upon the blot which we have left upon an other-
wise spotless reputation. I sincerely believe that
I utter the voice of the people of Massachusetts
on this matter, who, without distinction of party,
respect a great and good man. I trust that,
after the explanation I have made, it will be
found that I have set forth views which, if not
entirely acceptable to the loyal soldiers of the
nation, will at least be borne by them with kindness and with consideration for their advocate
and friend, for whom I speak. But however this
may be, I speak for myself honestly and sincerely, and with a warm desire to express the grati-
tude I feel to one who has differed from me in
a manly and magnanimous way, and who has
agreed and sympathized with me without cavil or
suspicion. There are periods in the life of every
man, when a generous act or word takes a place
which can never be forgotten. There are sudden
and impulsive expressions of kindness, which are
accepted as the genuine character of him who
utters them. For this, in addition to what I have

so abundantly offered, I stand here to speak for our senator; for this, and for that majestic appeal on his behalf made to me by that great man who has just passed away from us, and who carried with him those attributes of wisdom, and gentleness, and generosity, and honor, which when combined, inspire all our admiration and command all our obedience. I am confident, sir, that I have done my duty, feebly and imperfectly, but still with an approving conscience, and an earnest desire. And I trust the clear and conclusive report of the committee will be accepted, and that the Resolve presented by them will be passed as the sense of this legislature.